# WORD QUEST

by

Dr. Michael Thomson

with illustrations by
Margaret Woodhouse

Learning Development Aids

Word Quest is an exciting adventure in which you are the star of the story. During the quest, you will have to make many decisions. You will need to choose your own route to the Island of Words, and pick a safe pathway across the Syllable Swamp.

You will have to choose the right means of combat to fend off the many strange and dangerous creatures that you will meet. Keep all your wits about you as they will try and trick you and a mistake or wrong decision could cost you your life! Be warned adventurer, many terrible dangers await you and you will need to concentrate hard if you are to dodge the mad Consonant Dogs, avoid the perils of the Snake Pit and finally conquer the mighty Evil Wizard.

On your journey you will find some who are willing to help you, and you will also gather some very useful equipment. This will be very important to you if you are to complete the quest. Keep an equipment list, and collect as much as you can. Be careful not to waste any of your equipment at the wrong time. Sometimes you may not have the right equipment. You may have missed it and will need to go back.

To begin the quest, start at number one. From then on you will be told what to do. You may find it useful to write the numbers of the pages you go to on a piece of paper. Then if you make a mistake and get killed you will be able to go back to where you were and try again. You will have learned from your mistakes.

*Good luck brave adventurer – read on!*

# Part I   The Island of Words

## 1.

You are in a wood. You have to find the way in the wood. It is dark and cold. Only by following the vowels can you see the path. Put a pencil mark around the vowels:

| | | | | | | | |
|---|---|---|---|---|---|---|---|
| a | d | r | q | s | p | o | d |
| s | i | p | l | m | e | n | g |
| c | l | e | n | u | t | p | r |
| d | m | l | u | t | z | v | w |
| z | s | k | i | r | c | g | d |
| h | r | w | a | m | b | s | y |

If you made a Y shape – Go to 2.
If you made any other shape – try again!

## 2.

You travel north along a path. The trees thin out. You are in a space in the trees. A bow and arrow lies in front of you. The arrows have heads shaped like vowels. You hear barking. From behind the trees leap MAD CONSONANT DOGS. They have no vowels. You can stop them if you shoot them with vowels.

Write vowels in the spaces between the consonants to make real words. For example c t becomes cat, cot or cut.

c_____t        m_____g

t_____n        z_____p

c_____p        p_____t

If you made 6 real words – 13.
If not – 21.

# 3.

Your amazing accuracy and speed has succeeded in driving a prefix arrow into the heart of each HARPY. They fall screeching to their deaths, clawing uselessly at the arrows stuck in their breasts. You pass on shaken but determined to see your quest through – 138.

# 4.

The breath is squeezed out of you and you hear your ribs crack. Then blackness. You die! Back to 165 and try again!

# 5.

The blasts of SUFFIX energy beat against you and you lose all memory. You are absorbed by the wizard.

A terrible shame to fail so near the end of the adventure – back to 68 and try again.

# 6.

What spell will you use? Look at your equipment list to check that you have the spell you need. If you have not go to 218.

Vowel Sound Chart  –  50.
Magic e Oil  –  10.
Wall Blend Spell  –  146.

Remember to write down this page number (6), so that you can come back here if you choose the wrong spell.

# 7.

The Tree moans in anger. The roots shake and wrap around you. They squeeze tight. You are crushed to death. Bad luck! Back to 35 and try again.

## 8.

You beat at the monster with your syllable sticks. All to no effect, although wounded the gaping mouth swallows you up.

To start again look at 77, then back to 113.

## 9.

Oh, dear! you seem doomed to be lost in the swamp forever. You had better consult your syllable sticks(77) and try again – 134.

## 10.

You take the Magic e oil and rub it well into the planks. With a flash they get longer, like this

mat  →  mate

Now you must make the others longer, by adding Magic e and reading the words.

| | |
|---|---|
| win_____ | slop_____ |
| grim_____ | cut_____ |
| mop_____ | plum_____ |

If you've got all the words correct – 81.
If you did not – 147.

## 11.

The wizard reels back from your blows! His eyes widen in shock as he realises the power and the strength of your sword which has absorbed all the powers of the words you have learnt in the adventure. In one last desperate effort he casts out the letters

n  i  t  i  d  a  y  r  c  o

This is the spell that contains the secret of all the words in the world. If you can, rearrange those letters to make a word that you can use to neutralise the spell. Write the word here.

_____

You must not fail.

If you are right – 223.
If you fail you die together with the wizard!

## 12.

You walk back up the hill away from the swamp. You arrive back in the wood, near the shrine. Your mission has failed unless you return to the swamp (88).

## 13.

The dogs leap at you. You fire your arrows with speed. The dogs are all killed or run away. You are safe.

You may travel North, along the path leading from the space – 167.
You may go East, out to a field – 40.

## 14.

The witch is very nice. She gives you tea and then a small bottle marked "Magic e Oil". You take the bottle (Write down "Magic e Oil" on your Equipment List). and go on – 31.

## 15.

The path cuts straight on through the cliff. It ends in a clearing surrounded on all sides by cliffs. The cliffs are dark and gloomy. Suddenly, from the cliffs, rush large creatures giving out a high pitched (e) noise! They are HOMOPHONE BATS, common to this area.

over →

You can escape by filling in these sentences with the correct word.

1. We went to _____ in a boat. (see or sea)

2. We arranged to _____ him in the park. (meet or meat)

3. It was a tremendous _____ of daring. (feet or feat)

4. The bucket sprang a _____ (leek or leak)

5. The knife was made from stainless _____ (steal or steel)

If you got the words correct – 87.
If you made a mistake – 159.


## 16.

You take the left path. This gradually slopes down until you are in a gloomy passage under the mountain. This opens into a dark cave. You hear a loud (ā) sound. It gets louder and louder until it is almost unbearable. You are in one of the dreaded homophone traps. You can only escape by filling in these sentences with the correct word:

1. We _____ away in our boat. (sail or sale)

2. The lion had a golden _____ (mane or main)

3. The _____ laid the table for tea. (made or maid)

4. The huge _____ surfaced near the ship. (whale or wail)

5. The horse had a long _____ (tale or tail)

If you got all the words correct – 87.
If you made a mistake – 54.


## 17.

You overbalance and fall to your death! Poor fool!
(137 and choose again)

You cast the Wall Blend Spell. The end wall shakes and bits of brick come loose. Some of the bricks have -dge and -tch on. Other bricks have -ge and -ch on them. On the side wall a message in ghostly writing appears. It says "stop the vowel saying its name (long) by using the wall blends that are written on the bricks".

Use the bricks to fill in the following sentences:
Add -dge or -ge in sentences 1 and 2
Add -tch or -ch in sentences 3 and 4.

Copy out numbers 2 and 3. They will give you clues for later on.

1.   The hu_____ monkey sat on a le_____ in a ca_____.

2.   When you go across the bri_____ look under the he_____.

3.   Do not rea_____ for the pa_____ of bir_____ in the di_____.

4.   Swi_____ on the light, I do not have a ma_____ or a tor_____.

If you built the sentences correctly with the bricks – 102.
If not try again.

Out leap ghostly shapes. They are vowel GHOULS. They are spirits who for ever must moan until they find the sound that is right for them. They will take you into their spirit world unless you can help them. You must show them their vowels.

Look at the words. Find the vowels in each word and write them next to the word. One has been done for you.

| | | |
|---|---|---|
| mad  _a_ | top ____ | wet ____ |
| sad ____ | mug ____ | dog ____ |
| ten ____ | win ____ | bun ____ |
| pig ____ | | |

Now write two sentences using some of these words.

1.   ...................................................................................

2.   ...................................................................................

If you got the vowels right – 132.
If not – 73.

## 20.

You should have written plural water. Now you can add the correct endings to make these words plural.

cat_____ hand_____ lamp_____

car_____ hat_____ clock_____

If you were correct – 55.
If you made mistakes – try again!

## 21.

The dogs leap at you. Oh, dear! They tear your throat out and you die! (Start again).

## 22.

Look at the map of the Island of Words. You are in the town.

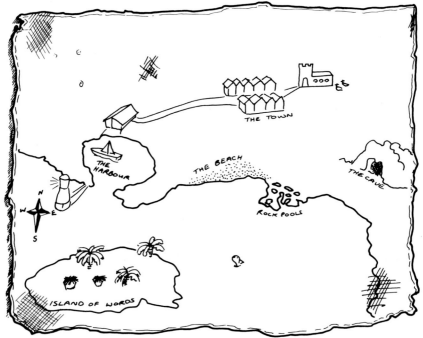

Now go to 24.

## 23.

As you wade across the stream a shoal of PIRHANAS go for your feet. You kick out and run. They bite at you. Can you run so fast that you escape? Test your speed. Use a stopwatch, or a friend to time you saying the following letters out aloud. Say the letter names.

b q p d g h y m n o u a i e

If you say the letters in less than 10 secs – 44.
If you say the letters in more than 10 secs – 65.

## 24.

It is busy in the town, you are keen to explore.

Where will you go?
The Harbour – 57
The Beach – 66

## 25.

The house and the witch fade to nothing. You hear laughter. You go on – 31.

## 26.

You cannot get in until you have paid the fee. You will have to do them again until you get them right – 57.

## 27.

The smell of the flowers puts you to sleep. You are in a magic sleep. You will sleep for ever. Only a frog can help you. It must kiss you. But there are no frogs. You must go back to 40 and try again.

## 28.

You set off to the rock pools. The tide starts to come in. You may drown! You must stand on rocks to be saved! Do this by putting a circle round the vowels.

l   k   a   n   q   e   r   s

z   d   u   i   v   b   o   c

If you were right – 30.
If you made a mistake, you drown! Better do them again.

## 29.

The PHANTOM looms over you; his icy breath freezes your bones. The chill takes all the warmth and life from you. You die a cold death! Back to 164.

## 30.

You are at the rock pools. You look into the pools and see consonant blends. You see

| | | |
|---|---|---|
| cr crab | st star | br brush |
| sp spade | sn snake | gr grape |
| ch chip | sh ship | dr drum |

You may take four of these blends. Think about which of the things will be of most use to you in your quest. Write them on your equipment list.

Now you may go on to the cave – 45 or go back to town – 22.

## 31.

You hear a "cr, cr, sp, sp" noise in the trees. All around, from the trees, drop big CONSONANT CROWS and SPIDER BLENDS. They peck and bite at you.

Your only hope is to get them to eat each other and make words. Match them up, add any vowel, and try to make as many real words as possible. 'Crows' at the front of the words and 'spiders' at the end, so fr + e + sh is fresh and fr + o + st is frost. – See page 11 (opposite).

| Crows | Spiders |
|-------|---------|
| fr | st |
| br | ng |
| fl | sh |
| cr | nd |

fresh _____ _____
frost _____ _____

_____ _____ _____

_____ _____ _____

_____ _____ _____

_____ _____ _____

_____ _____ _____

_____ _____ _____

_____ _____ _____

_____ _____ _____

If you made 8 or 9 real words – 92.
If you made 10 or more real words – 56.
If you made 7 or less real words – 39.

You walk down the road and come to a town. You see an old man. He has a map. He wants to sell it to you. Will you –

Buy the map – 47.
Try and steal the map – 49.
Walk on – 59.

You hear the sound of beating drums coming from the swamp. The beats are syllables (the beats in words). Before you can enter the swamp you must reply to the swamp drums. You do this by beating with your syllable sticks on a hollow log. You beat out these words by dividing them into their syllables or beats. The first two are done for you:

| | |
|---|---|
| acorn | a'corn |
| September | Sep'tem'ber |
| underneath | _____ |
| railway | _____ |
| magnificent | _____ |

When you have done these, and corrected them (if you made mistakes), you may go on! – 85.

To help the crab you need to sort these words into the right vowel families. The first two have been done for you. (The crab knows where these two are!).

mad, hop, fed, big, pig, cup, can, bin, ten, bun, pot, sit, pet, tap, ham, get, dog, nut, box, hug.

| a | e | i | o | u |
|---|---|---|---|---|
| mad | _____ | _____ | hop | _____ |
| _____ | _____ | _____ | _____ | _____ |
| _____ | _____ | _____ | _____ | _____ |
| _____ | _____ | _____ | _____ | _____ |

If you got 17–20 correct – 82.
If you got 16 or less correct – 36.

You edge up to the tree. A huge face appears in the tree trunk, and roots shake and rise out from the ground. The tree lumbers out of the earth towards you. It is the TREE OF SYLLABLE KNOWLEDGE. A creaky voice says "Feed my roots and you can take my sticks. Fail and my roots will crush you".

You must put a ring round the 'c' in the words, if the 'c' says (s).

| | | | | |
|---|---|---|---|---|
| city | cat | cube | cycle | celery |
| cable | circus | crab | prince | can |
| recent | centre | civil | cyclone | cent |

If you picked out all the soft c's – 61.
If you failed – 7.

## 36.

Oh dear! You can't seem to find all the little crabs. The big crab is angry! It has lots of friends. They pinch you with their huge claws. It will be a painful death! Back to 34 and look at the vowels carefully!

## 37.

The sword lifts from the shrine and you take the hilt. It feels warm and powerful in your hand. The blade is made of finely forged steel. It is black with red letters or 'runes' on the blade. The runes say "Suffix Rule Sword: He who draws me will have the power of the demon SUFFIX. But let the owner beware. The demon may devour you if the rules are not used with care".

Keep the sword, you may have need of it. Write it on your equipment list. Take note of the warning – 84.

## 38.

You do not go into the cave.
You may go to:-
1. the Rock Pools – 30.
2. back to Town – 22.

## 39.

Some of the spiders and crows eat each other. The others go for you! There is a crunching sound. It is your bones being chewed! Hurry back to 31 to make up some more words before you are eaten!

## 40.

You go out into the field. You see flowers. The flowers give off a sickly smell. They have th, ch, sh and wh flower heads. You must pick only those that make question words. The others will put you to sleep. If you can't think of six try looking up "wh" in a dictionary.

Write them down.

_____

_____

_____

_____

_____

_____

If you wrote 6 question words go to – 52.
If not – 27.

## 41.

You walk into the cave. It is very dark and you cannot see. How
will you find your way? You must light up the cave by a lamp.

Put in -mp or -nd to make real words.

la _____

li _____

ha _____

du _____

me _____

If you made 5 real words – 131.
If you made less than 5 – 43.

## 42.

You look into the ditch. A clawed hand reaches out. You hear a
grating sneer "You were warned, foolish one!" You are pulled into the
ditch – 222.

## 43.

You lose your way in the cave. You see daylight to your left. You
walk towards it and find yourself back at Town – 22.

## 44.

Well done! Now you can speed across the stream like a streak of lightning – 154.

## 45.

In the side of the cliff is a deep cave. It is dark inside.

Will you go in? – Yes 41.
– No 38.

## 46.

As you finish you notice the remains of a human skeleton.

Go and investigate – 158.

## 47.

You check your equipment list. If you have any gold you can buy the map. You give the old man the gold (cross it off your equipment list) and take the map – 22. If you have no gold you must start again. (This time make sure that you write everything that you are given on your equipment list.)

## 48.

If you choose anything else apart from the Bow and Prefix arrows – 17.

If you choose the Bow and Prefix arrows – 162.

## 49.

The old man yells "Help! Thief!" The police come and you are put in jail for theft. To get out you must pay a fine of gold. If you have gold pay the fine, buy a map and go to 22. If you have no gold you must start again, and make sure that you write everything you are given on your equipment list.

## 50.

You open the vowel sound chart.

| Sound | Middle of words | End of words |
|---|---|---|
| ($\bar{a}$) | maid | play |
| ($\bar{i}$) | light | fly |
| ($\bar{o}$) | boat | bow |
| ($\bar{u}$) | food | stew |

Spelling of Vowel Sounds

As well as the above ancient spells, know also O Reader.

| | | |
|---|---|---|
| (ow) | sound | cow |
| (oi) | boil | toy |
| (or) | August | saw |

Now turn back to the page you were on. Use the ancient knowledge! (If it is right for your task of course!)

## 51.

You give the old man your gold and take the map – 22.

## 52.

You find a path in the field. Go to 167.

## 53.

With crows at the front of the word and spiders at the end, add vowels and match the blends eg fr + e + sh is fresh. This time you must make at least 10 real words including the examples.

| Crows | Spiders | | | |
|-------|---------|------|------------|------------|
| fr | st | e.g. | frost | _____ |
| br | ng | | fresh | _____ |
| cr | nd | | _____ | _____ |
| | | | _____ | _____ |
| | | | _____ | _____ |

When you have made 10 real words, you have earned the wall blend spell. Write it on your equipment list and go back to 148.

## 54.

The noise rises and deafens you. Horrible noisy creatures leap out. You are driven mad by their continual (ā) and become a Homophone yourself. Go back to 16 and try again.

-18-

# Part II   The Syllable Swamp

This is Part 2 of Word Quest. You should have finished Part 1, and are at the Island of Words.

**To show that you have finished Part 1** you must use what you found in the chest on the Island of Words. Write down the treasure here.

_____

You must use it to make these words plural. Scatter the water on the words to make plurals.

   <u>dog</u>    <u>man</u>    chair    <u>duck</u>

If you were correct read on. If not make corrections and then read on.

You need to check your equipment list now to see that will help you. It would also be a good idea to go over and remember what has happened in Part 1. Now you can explore. You see that there is a lovely garden behind you.

Will you enter? – 170.

### 56.

A flash of light! You have rescued the Wizard blend from crows and spiders. He is so grateful that he gives you a magic spell. It is a "WALL BLEND SPELL". Keep it, write it on your equipment list, and go to 92.

### 57.

You go to the harbour. You must pay a fee to get in. You must write in the correct words to make the sentences.

The dog bit the _____.    (man cup)

A fox ate the _____.    (hen zip)

The rat _____ in the bin          (hat hid)

The pig is in the _____.          (cup mud)

Dan put _____ on the bun.          (jam fat)

If you got them all right – 62.
If you made a mistake – 26.

## 58.

A flash of lightning and clap of thunder and the "W Witch" (that is who it was) disappears in a cloud of smoke. Cackling laughter reaches your ears – 124.

## 59.

You walk on into the town. It looks like a maze. Where will you go now? Back to 32, before you get lost!

## 60.

You step onto one of the pits, and fall into the pit of snakes. Your only hope is to scramble out before the snakes bite. It will not be easy! Test your speed. Use a stopwatch or friend, to time you. Say the following letters (sounds please!)

u, o, r, w, b, d, p, t, g, c, e, i, a

If you said them correctly in less than 8 seconds – 216.
If you take more than 8 seconds or got any wrong – 103.

## 61.

"Ah, that's better! My roots are well fed. Well done. Now take my sticks". You take the coloured sticks. They may be looked at whenever you wish at 77. (Write syllable sticks on your equipment list and note the page number so that you don't forget).

Put the sticks away, thank the tree, and return to the path – 101.

## 62.

You walk into the harbour. You see many ships. The Island of Words can be seen far away. Check your equipment list. If you have a ship blend you can take a ship and sail away – 64.

If you do not have a ship blend you must go to the beach and get one! – 66 (Try visiting the rock pool).

## 63.

You grasp the sword hilt. The deep hum turns to a moan. You hear a voice:

"This sword is to add endings to words. You must prove your skill, mortal, before you can wield it!"

The words shown below have been sliced in two by the sword. You must put the correct two pieces together to make real words, e.g. armchair. You must not fail!

| | | |
|------|-------|----------------|
| arm  | file  | armchair |
| tea  | path  | |
| rain | chair | |
| sky  | band  | |
| head | line  | |
| nail | spoon | |
| foot | coat  | |

If you make the correct words – 37.
If you fail – 168.

## 64.

You take a ship and sail towards the Island of Words. As you sail a storm comes. Thunder and Lightning! Can you escape? You must find a way and stop the boat from sinking. You can do this by finding the correct spellings. You will need the Storm Spelling Rule Scroll. If you have not got it, go back and search on the beach – 66. If you have the Storm Spelling Rule Scroll you may go to 78.

# 65.

Your feet can't pick up speed. You feel the PIRHANAS bite into them. The pain makes you fall. The fish eat you with savage speed. Try using the bridge – 152.

# 66.

Before you can get to the beach, you must write out the alphabet underneath.

---

---

If you are correct move to 67.
If not try again.

# 67.

You are on a wide, sandy beach with rock pools by the sea. You see a huge crab coming towards you. To your surprise it speaks!

"Will you help me find my family of little crabs?"

Will you help?   Yes – 34.
                 No – 72.

# 68.

You must have guessed it! Correct! The Suffix Rule Sword. You draw it from its sheath (unless, that is, you are foolish enough to have used it at the END PASSAGE. In which case you have no sword and die immediately!)

As the fine blade of the sword is drawn, a rich humming fills the air. The runes or rules on the blade of the sword glow in gold. It says: "Words of one syllable, with one vowel ending in one consonant, double the consonant if the suffix begins with a vowel."

You parry the wizard's first blast and attack with the sword. You must complete the following (The first is done for you. Note – y on its own acts as a vowel).

| | | |
|---|---|---|
| shop+ed | = | shopped |
| hop+ing | = | _____ |
| swim+ing | = | _____ |
| grim+ly | = | _____ |
| hum+ed | = | _____ |
| grit+y | = | _____ |
| spoon+ful | = | _____ |
| grin+ing | = | _____ |
| slim+ed | = | _____ |

7 or 8 correct – 157.
6 or less correct – 5.

## 69.

You use the lamp to see. You find another bottle of Magic e oil. Keep it, (write it down on your equipment list).

You can go to the Rock Pools – 28, or Town – 22.

## 70.

You fall off the bridge, and splash into the stream.
You stand up – 23.

## 71.

You hold on to the log and are tossed about. After a while you land on the same river bank. You are tired out. You fall into a deep sleep. When you wake up, use Magic e oil to make all the planks longer – 10.

## 72.

The crab attacks you! It has a lot of friends. They attack you too. You run away back to town – 22.

The moaning gets louder "ooooh". You become a vowel GHOUL. You will moan forever, unless you can find the vowels – 19 and try again! (Hint: look at the middle of each word).

## 74.

You must use all the oil to open the chest. Cross it off your equipment list. You see a note inside the chest. It says "Vowels can be long (say their name), or short (say their sound). You can use sound pictures to show the vowels, 'a' can be (ă), the short or vowel sound, or (ā) the long or vowel name. 'Magic e' makes the vowel sound long".

Make these vowels long. Write the new word and vowel sound picture.

| e.g. | tap | tape | (ā) |
|------|-----|--------|------|
|      | hat | _____ | ____ |
|      | win | _____ | ____ |
|      | tub | _____ | ____ |
|      | mop | _____ | ____ |

Now write spellings of these sound pictures.

| e.g. | (rīp) | ripe |
|------|-------|--------|
|      | (cūb) | _____ |
|      | (măn) | _____ |
|      | (tĭp) | _____ |
|      | (lāt) | _____ |
|      | (hōp) | _____ |

7–9 correct – 86
0–6 correct – 76

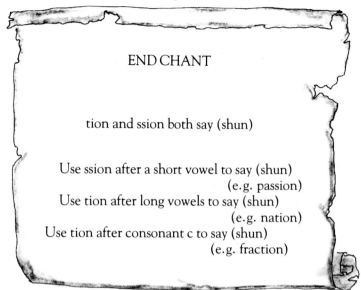

## END CHANT

tion and ssion both say (shun)

Use ssion after a short vowel to say (shun)
(e.g. passion)
Use tion after long vowels to say (shun)
(e.g. nation)
Use tion after consonant c to say (shun)
(e.g. fraction)

Now return to the page you were on.

## 76.

Oh dear! You are doomed to sit on the island forever. Look out for sand flies, they get a pest after 50 years! 74 for another try.

THE SYLLABLE STICKS. You have two syllable sticks of different colours, as follows:

Red stick – closed syllables – The vowel is closed by a consonant at the end. A consonant, or more than one, follows the vowel. The vowel is closed in and says its short sound.

For example:    let,    fun,    mag'net

Green stick – open syllables – The vowel is not closed in, but can say its name. One vowel is at the end. The vowel is normally long.

For example:    me,    to,    Fi'do

You will need to use these sticks to analyse words. So, for example,

'napkin' can be split into two closed syllables – năp'kĭn. The letter 'c' goes over the syllable to mean closed. The word label has one open and one closed syllable – lā'bĕl. The letter "o" means an open syllable.

More examples:    Velvet    – vĕl'vĕt

Student    – stū'dĕnt

Gravy    – grā'vȳ (y acts as a vowel)

Dentist    – dĕn'tĭst

You will need to use these sticks later! Now turn back to the place you were.

Look at the Storm Spelling Rule Scroll on your equipment list (93). Now put a circle around the wrong spellings. Then write them out correctly.

| kis | hit | fill | then | til |
|-----|-----|------|------|-----|
| mis | mess | stuf | pram | gruff |
| hul | wish | hiss | wil | hill |

_____  _____  _____  _____  _____

_____  _____

If you got 5 or 6 correct – 95
If you made 2 or more mistakes – 80

## 79.

You dive into the river. You swim as fast as you can, but the current is too strong. You are swept downstream. You see a log. It has the word SAVE on it. Is the 'A' in save, a long or short vowel? Write down the sound picture, or write down 'long' or 'short'.

If you are correct – 71
If you are wrong – 128.

## 80.

The wind turns the boat over. The storm has sunk you. You drown – not a nice end! Look again at the Storm Spelling Rule Scroll (93) and go back to 78.

## 81.

You place the planks across the river. They are long enough to make a bridge. You walk over in safety. A path leads to a road. You have no magic e oil left now. Cross it off your equipment list. You may need to find some more later. There is a sign "To the Island of Words". Will you go on? – 32.

## 82.

The crab is very pleased. It gives you a piece of paper. It is a scroll. To read it go to 93 then return here.

Now you can go to

1. The Rock Pools – 28.
2. The Cave – 45.

You walk over to the hedge and brush aside the leaves. There is an old box with the letter "W" imprinted in gold on the top. Under the sign is written "Warning: Phonic clues".

Will you open the box? – 90
Rejoin the path? – 99.

You continue along the woodland path. It is nearing night and you are hungry and thirsty. You need shelter for the night. The path ahead opens to a road and you see a castle at the end of the road. It is dark and gloomy, but you see a light shining beyond the gate. The road branches here, one fork leads into the castle, the other curves around and leads on to the mountains in the distance.

Will you enter the castle? – 165.
Carry on around the castle? – 91.

You enter the swamp. The air smells like rotten eggs and twisted branches crouch over you like vultures. You can see the path winding over solid grass lumps with the stinking slime-covered water to each side. As you walk along, your feet sink into the grass for a few inches. The path curves around a huge mangrove tree; you hear a horrible roaring noise that shakes the ground. You turn the corner and there is the huge SYLLABLE MONSTER. He is a massive, green scaly thing. Its mouth OPENS and CLOSES. Words can be seen on its sharp teeth. You have no choice but to fight the monster. What will you use?

Suffix Rule Sword   – 160.
Wall Blend Spell   – 151.
Magic W Spell   – 151.
Syllable Sticks   – 214.

# THE SYLLABLE SWAMP

# 86.

You open the chest! You find a message and a small bottle. The bottle is labelled "Plural Water". The message says "Welcome to the Island of Words". Write plural water on your equipment list.

You have done well and the first adventure ends. But now you can explore the Island! For this you can go to part 2. when you are ready – 55.

# 87.

You quickly retrace your steps to reach the crossroads – 155. Chant the end chant as you go so that you can choose between the three paths again.

# 88.

The road winds down a hill. The plants take on a lush green colour. As you walk on, the air becomes damp. The ground underfoot is soft. You are entering the SYLLABLE SWAMP!

Will you go on?
If you do – 33
If you do not – 12

# 89.

You dig! You find a chest. You try to open the chest. It is stuck. You see a message on the lid. It says 'To open me, rub magic e oil over my lid'. Check your equipment. Do you have any Magic e oil?

Yes – 74
No – 166

You open the box. Inside is a scroll. You read: "This box contains a PHONIC ANALYSIS KIT, and some Magic W Spells". You can examine the Phonic Analysis Kit at any time (Go to 117). You can use the spells when you are given a choice. Write down phonic analysis kit and the page number (117) as well as W spells on your equipment list. Go to 99.

## 91.

You walk along the road. Night falls and it is cold. You are faint with hunger and thirst. You fall to the ground with tiredness. Your only hope is to return to the castle before you die. You rise to your feet and stagger back. – 165.

## 92.

The vile spiders and crows have eaten each other. Ugh! What a meal! You are safe. The path goes on past an old barn. It is getting dark. The night is cold. Do you:

Go into the barn for the night – 110
Go on down the road – 120.

## 93.

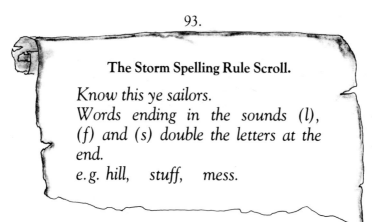

**The Storm Spelling Rule Scroll.**

*Know this ye sailors.*
*Words ending in the sounds (l),*
*(f) and (s) double the letters at the*
*end.*
*e.g. hill,    stuff,    mess.*

Copy this onto your equipment list, it may be very useful later. Now go back to – 82.

## 94.

You rush to the wall. You try and climb up. There are no footholds. You break a fingernail. It hurts! – 170.

## 95.

You find your way. You see the Island ahead and land. You look at the map and find the place marked X. It probably means that there is buried treasure. You need a spade! Check your equipment. This will be the sp spade consonant blend.

If you do not have a spade – 107.
If you do – 89

## 96.

You wisely walk on and into the wood. As you pass by you notice that one of the trees has a number of coloured sticks hanging from a branch. These bang together in the wind making a strange sound. It is as if they say "Take,,k,k,k us,s,s".

You go towards the tree – 35.

## 97.

The path leads you out onto rocky ground, which gradually rises. You find yourself entering a narrow pass between two large hills; each side of you a rocky wall rises sheer and unclimbable. Gradually the path narrows until it appears to end in a smooth wall.

It is the END PASSAGE. There does not appear to be any way forward. What will you do? You can use

Wall blend spell – 118
Phonic Analysis Kit – 150
Suffix Rule Sword – 116
End Chant – 144.

## 98.

Well done! You have found your way out! You have now completed Part 2 of Word Quest! The Syllable Swamp is behind you. When you are ready you can go on to Part 3 – 100.

## 99.

You walk ahead down the path. You come to a gate leading out of the garden. It is the only way out. Leaning on the gate is an old woman. She wears a tall black hat with the letter W on it. She laughs and says

"You cannot pass the gate
It is your fate
But I change the vowel
And you must howl"

What will you do?
You can charge at the
old woman and try and
knock her out of the way – 58.
Look at your equipment list – 114.

## 100.

# Part III:    The Encounter with the Wizard

This is the third and final part of your quest. Once again you will need to check your equipment list, and also remind yourself of what has gone on before in The Island of Words and The Syllable Swamp. You will need all your skill, and some luck, if you are to defeat the terrible might of the Wizard.

After you have rested and gathered energy for the journey you set off. As if in protest against the damp slime of the Swamp the land becomes dry and barren. Here and there you see evidence of the terrible destruction of the Wizard. The land has been laid waste. The trees are stark against the skyline, the fields blackened. This is indeed a bleak place. You hurry on to 97.

## 101.

You walk on into the wood. The trees and bushes grow closer together here. The trees shut out the light. The path twists and turns. It becomes very narrow. You can hardly find your way. You hear a low moaning (ā), (ē), (ī), (ō), (ū). You are in the vowel digraph maze!

You can continue through the maze and try and find a way out – 127

Try and force your way out of the wood through the tangle of thorn bushes – 169.

## 102.

You have taken out enough bricks to make a hole in the wall. As you start to crawl in, the wall opens up into an archway. You walk into an area with trees and flowers laid out in long rows. A bridge crosses a small stream. It has no side rail and is very narrow.

You can try to cross the bridge – 152.
You can wade across – 23.

## 103.

Oh dear! You only get halfway out and a snake bites you on the ankle. You die of vowel sound poisoning (you had better go back to 101 and try again).

## 104

The PHANTOM says "You must choose the spellings for (cher), (shun) and (er) that are given. These must be matched to the correct beginnings to make real words". Choose any right ending to make one word for each of the beginnings.

| Beginnings | Endings | Real words |
|---|---|---|
| Sta | ture | _____ |
| vineg | | _____ |
| punc | tion | _____ |
| cap | | _____ |
| popula | ar | _____ |
| lec | | _____ |
| frac | | _____ |
| peculi | | _____ |
| pic | | _____ |
| rela | | _____ |

If you are correct – 122.
If you make mistakes – 29.

## 105.

You strike out with your stick. The monster howls and after drawing back lunges forward and attacks. You have chosen only one kind of syllable stick. You still have time to use the correct stick. Next time you may not be so lucky – 214.

## 106.

You die a horrible, choking death!

## 107.

You must find a spade. To do so you will have to go back across the sea in your ship. Do you remember where to find the consonant blends? – Try the rock pools – 28.

## 108.

Nothing happens – 114.

## 109.

The GUARDIAN crushes you with his huge arms. You cannot move. You feel the breath being squeezed out of you. Your only hope is to try and trip him into the moat. To do this you must rearrange these letters to make a ph (sounding f) word. Clue: another name for a ghost. OMTANHP

_____

If you are correct – 139.
If you fail – 4.

## 110.

You go into the barn. It is dark. You lie on the straw to keep warm. You hear a noise. A moaning "oooh" and "aaah" – 19.

## 111.

The moaning rises to a shriek. You clap your hands over your ears! Too late, your brain is bursting! Go to 127 to try again.

Get help from your phonic analysis kit (117) and vowel sound chart (50). Make a note of the page number 127 first.

## 112.

The thorn bushes close in on you. They bite into your skin. What a horrible death! Back to 169 to try again. A Sound Spelling Dictionary will help, if you have one (or get help!).

You take the red and green sticks together. Take note of what the sticks say (go to 77 if you need to). The monster bares its teeth. You need to divide the words you see on the teeth into open and closed syllables. The first two have been done by some other adventurer. c = closed o = open

| | |
|---|---|
| pistol | $\overset{\text{c}}{\text{pis}}\text{'}\overset{\text{c}}{\text{tol}}$ |
| open | $\overset{\text{o}}{\text{o}}\text{'}\overset{\text{c}}{\text{pen}}$ |
| magnet | _____ |
| final | _____ |
| stupid | _____ |
| tennis | _____ |
| evil | _____ |
| infant | _____ |
| robot | _____ |
| silent | _____ |
| spider | _____ |
| cupid | _____ |

If you got 8 or more correct – 119
If you got 7 or less correct – 8.

You can use any of the spells listed below but before you go on, make a note of this page number so that you know where to come back to if you choose a spell that is of no use to you.

Magic e oil          – 108
Wall Blend Spell     – 108
Phonic Analysis Kit – 117
Magic W Spells       – 135.

If you do not have the right spell you have missed it. Re-trace your steps along the path until you find the hedge – 83.

Write down the words that mean the following. The first one is done for you. All use 'ph' saying (f) spellings.

A name: <u>Philip</u>.

Something a camera helps you make:  _____

An animal with a long trunk: _____

Short for an instrument you talk into and listen to. It lets you talk to people who are a long way away:  _____

All the letters are called the:  _____

If you get these words right, and spell them correctly – 139.
If you make a mistake – 109.

You draw out your Suffix Rule Sword and smash it against the rock wall. The sword breaks; the wall remains. Oh dear! You might need that sword later.

You throw away the shattered remains – 97 and choose again.

You open the phonic analysis kit. It will help with some problems. Inside are sets of diacritical marks – breves and macrons. Also are numerous sets of brackets for making sound pictures. The guide book says:

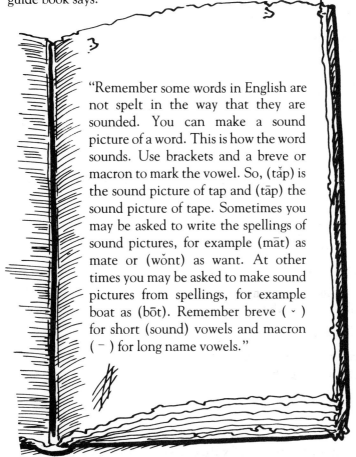

"Remember some words in English are not spelt in the way that they are sounded. You can make a sound picture of a word. This is how the word sounds. Use brackets and a breve or macron to mark the vowel. So, (tăp) is the sound picture of tap and (tāp) the sound picture of tape. Sometimes you may be asked to write the spellings of sound pictures, for example (māt) as mate or (wŏnt) as want. At other times you may be asked to make sound pictures from spellings, for example boat as (bōt). Remember breve ( ˘ ) for short (sound) vowels and macron ( ¯ ) for long name vowels."

Now turn back to the page you were on.

118.

You cast the spell. The wall wavers but does not disappear. Obviously this END wall is not made of "wall words". – 97 and choose again.

## 119.

The monster screams in agony. Your clever syllable division beats it to the ground. The beast thrashes around, but you avoid its huge body as it crashes to the ground, lifeless.

As a mark of your victory you draw your own syllable monster. Draw your monster in the space below or on a separate sheet. Use nonsense syllables to give it a name like a "Lig'u'ped". Anything you like, use as many syllables as you like. Then go to 46.

## 120.

You hurry down the road. From the barn you hear "oooh" and "aaah" – 19.

## 121.

The smoke thins out and blows away. So does the witch! You hear a WWW-wail as she is blown away on the wind. You walk through the gate and out into the wood again. There is a ditch running to one side. You hear a moaning sound "Help!" from the ditch. There is a patch of birch trees there.

Will you look into the ditch – 42
Carry on into the wood – 96.

## 122.

The PHANTOM fades away. You feel yourself becoming very sleepy. You fall into a deep sleep and wake the following morning outside on the road. The castle is no longer there. Was it a dream? Yet you feel refreshed and no longer hungry. In your hand is a note. It says

"You have met the challenge of the PHANTOM from END CASTLE and survived. You may have the END CHANT".

You find a scroll of paper in your other hand. It is the END CHANT. Write it down on your equipment list. You may look at this any time – make a note of the page number (75). For now you move on down the road feeling very happy – 88.

## 123.

Don't be silly! What spell does a wall need?
If you have a wall blend spell – 148.
If you have not got a wall blend spell –221.

## 124.

You seem to be stuck. The gate will not open. You fall into a trance and wake later – 114.

## 125.

Write down the words that mean the following. The first one is done for you. All use ch saying (k) spellings.

We give presents to others on this December day: <u>Christmas.</u>

A shop where you can buy Aspirin and other drugs: _____

A group of people singing together can be a: _____

A place where children go to work and play: _____

A group of people playing musical instruments together is an:

_____

If you get these words right and spell them correctly – 139.
If you make a mistake – 109.

126.

You cross the clearing safely. You walk on through the path in the wood. It is a bright, shiny day and the sun slants across the trees casting patches of light and shadow. You are enjoying your walk when to the right of the path you see a shrine lit up by the sunlight through the trees. The shrine is in a clearing which is peaceful and calm. You blink your eyes and seem to see a glint of metal and flash of jewels upon the shrine. What could it be? Is it something that will be useful to you later?

Will you visit the shrine and investigate – 143.
Walk on – 84.

## 127.

The maze is very complex. To get through the 'MOANING BUSHES' you need to complete the tables below. In the left hand table write in the sound picture, and in the right hand one write in the correct spelling.

| Spelling | Sound picture | Spelling | Sound picture |
|----------|---------------|----------|---------------|
| grain | _____ | _____ | (trān) |
| flight | _____ | _____ | (stā) |
| try | _____ | _____ | (flōt) |
| grow | _____ | | |
| meat | _____ | _____ | (flū) |

If you complete the table correctly – 161.
If not – 111.

## 128.

You grab the log and miss. You are pulled under water and start to drown. Quickly back to 142 and cast a spell to save yourself.

## 129.

You charge the gate. The wood crashes open and splinters fly in all directions. A hooded figure appears. "You dare to destroy and spoil the END CASTLE GATE. You were warned! Begone to limbo! You fade to nothing and die. Back to 139 and choose again!

## 130.

The HARPIES peck you to death. Better try again! (162).

The lamp you make lights up the cave. You see a dusty bottle. It is marked "Magic e oil". Write it on your equipment list. Now you can go to the rock pools – 28, or Town – 22.

## 132.

The vowel GHOULS stop moaning. In fact they are much more fun than you thought. They ask you to have dinner with them in the barn. They are so happy to be able to talk that they give you a VOWEL SOUND CHART. Write it on your equipment list. Keep it! They also give you a piece of gold. Write that on your equipment list also! – 142.

## 133.

Well done! You force your way through the MOANING BUSHES. You have managed to get past the first part of the "vowel digraph maze". You come out into another part of the wood – 161.

## 134.

The ground is quite firm under your feet, but you can see no way out. You realise that you face one of your most difficult tasks. You must escape this maze of syllables. The only way you can do this is to analyse the swamp. You will need both your syllable sticks to probe for solid ground, beat down the undergrowth and for word analysis. You may need to consult the sticks (77). Divide these words into syllables and show the type of syllable.

Note  o = open syllable
      c = closed syllable

The first two words have been done for you!

nutmeg     nut'meg (c,c)
November   No'vem'ber (o,c,c)

remember   _____

kingdom   _____

intending   _____

duet   _____

electric   _____

together   _____

consultant   _____

immortal   _____

September   _____

triumph   _____

economic   _____

dial   _____

torpedo   _____

comprehend   _____

These are not easy!

If you got 10 or more right –98.
If you got 5–9 correct – 153.
If you got less then 5 correct – 9.

## 135.

You cast the spells. The witch screams "Aha! You challenge my power. Take the W words then. I change the vowels!"

A deep voice fills your head. You hear

"The W witch can change sounds in vowels coming after W. These are the ways:

wa – a after W sounds like (ŏ) e.g. was (wŏs)
war – ar after W sounds like (or) e.g. war (wor)
wor – or after W sounds like (er) e.g. word (werd)

Now you can solve her riddle".

The witch claps her hands and clouds of smoke appear – 136.

In the smoke is written "Solve my riddle or die (werm)!"

You must write down the correct spellings of the sound pictures. The sound picture is what the word sounds like when you say it.

(wŏs) _____     (wŏnt) _____

(wor) _____     (wŏsh) _____

(worm) _____     (werm) _____

(werk) _____     (sworm) _____

If you are correct – 121.
If you make mistakes – 145.

137.

A path winds up the side of the mountain. You feel that you are nearing your destination. There is a feeling of tension in the air. The path narrows until you have only three feet upon which to walk. On one side steep cliffs, on the other a terrifying drop to jagged rocks at the mountain's foot. Just as you begin to get the hang of balancing you see small black dots appear in the sky. The dots get larger until screaming with fury, and with their beaks and talons slashing at you, the last of the mad wizard's creatures attack. They are the dreaded PREFIX HARPIES. Half eagle and half human they can tear your flesh apart, not to mention causing you to fall to your death. Check your equipment. What will you use to fight off the dreaded birds?

Write your choice here _____

Now go to 48.

## 138.

The narrow path leads to a cave perched high on the mountain. You enter the cave and see splendid and beautiful jewels, and, in caskets arrayed in fine coloured cloth, the other ill-gotten gains of the mad wizard – the words of the world. Will you be too late to save them? As you ponder the riches in awe, a mighty thunderclap sounds and before you, dressed in robes of deep purple covered in golden stars is the MAD WIZARD. This is your final and most deadly encounter. The wizard cackles insanely. "So, foolish one, you dare challenge my power. You shall die painfully!" So saying, he raises his arms and hurls a terrible blast of "MIXED SUFFIXES" at you. Is this the end? How will you counter the mad wizard? Check you equipment and go to 68.

## 139.

You link your legs around the back of the giant's ankle, and you both fall into the moat with a splash. You rise to the surface spitting out the foul green water. The GUARDIAN holds his belly and roars with laughter. "Ho! You fooled me, little one! You can now enter". With a grunt and a swing of his vast arm he hurls you out of the moat you find yourself standing outside the gate.

Will you charge down the gate with your shoulder – 129
Pull the lever that is set into the wall – 164.

## 140.

The wall is still in your way. You must use more bricks to make a way.

Use dge or ge tch or ch to complete the following:

| | |
|---|---|
| ju-_____ | tha-_____ |
| do-_____ | pea-_____ |
| frin-_____ | sti-_____ |
| hu-_____ | por-_____ |

If you finish these correctly – 102.
If not – 141.

# 141.

Oh dear! You are doomed to rot here forever! (Start Part 2 again!) – 55.

# 142.

You sleep in the barn with the vowel ghoul for the night.

In the morning you thank them for their kindness to you and set off down the road. You come to a river. There is no way to cross. You notice some planks. You lay them across the river. They are just too short. You notice words on the plank, like this:

```
+-----------------+
|                 |
|   m a t         |
|                 |
+-----------------+
```

You can try to swim the river – 79.
You can use a spell – 6.

# 143.

You near the shrine and hear a deep sound like "Ommm" in the air. A shaft of sunlight touches the shrine. You see a sword with a gold and ruby hilt sticking straight up from the shrine. You see writing at the foot of the shrine.

"He who takes this sword shall add an end without fear".

What can it mean?

You can take the sword – 63.
Return to the path – 84.

# 144.

You unroll the scroll with the End Chant (75). You read it out aloud in a clear voice. Parts of the words appear. You must add the spelling of the sound (shun) to the words. Use the End Chant to help. Some poor fool has done the first two for you. Hint – add (shun) and try the vowel long or short. Which is the *real* word? (Go to 75 to read the End Chant but remember to make a note of this page number first).

| | | | |
|---|---|---|---|
| loca | location | objec | _____ |
| percu | percussion | discu | _____ |
| expre | _____ | imita | _____ |
| genera | _____ | informa | _____ |
| infec | _____ | proce | _____ |
| irrita | _____ | | |

If you get the answers right – 155. Otherwise there will be no way forward. Re-do the words if you have made a mistake.

### 145.

The smoke becomes thicker. You choke as it gathers round you. You cannot breathe. Back to 136 and re-do the words before you die. Think of the spellings of the w words.

### 146.

You cast the spell. Nothing happens – back to 6 to choose again.

### 147.

Only some of the planks are long enough. Some fall into the river as you try to cross. You fall in. You see a log in the water – 71.

### 148.

Which spell will you use?

Magic e oil        – 123
Wall Blend Spell   – 18
Vowel Sound Chart– 123

Remember that you cannot use a spell that you haven't got on your equipment list. If you do not have the right spell – 221.

# 149.

Leaving your monster as a guide for future travellers you march on. The swamp gets thicker; the trees and muddy pools cover up the pathway. The tangle of roots and vegetation make it difficult to find your way. You are lost in the swamp. You see a gap in the trees to your right, and the way ahead seems clear. Which Way will you go?

Right – 215
Ahead – 134.

# 150.

You take out the phonic analysis kit and examine the wall for unusual sounds. You find a (shun) sound. Now what? – 97 and choose again.

# 151.

You cast your spell. Oh dear! Nothing happens! Your spells do not appear to have any effect on the syllable teeth. You are swallowed up. Bad luck! (Try again) – 85.

# 152.

You walk onto the bridge. You begin to lose your balance. Keep your balance by making a long pole from the words you find by using the vowel/blend patterns. Match up the letters with the endings. If you make a *real* word, write it down on the space.

| | | |
|---|---|---|
| h | ard | hard _____ |
| | arm | _____ |
| | ark | _____ |
| sh | ort | _____ |
| | irt | _____ |
| | art | _____ |

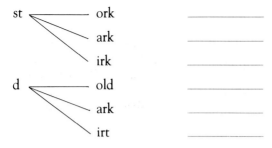

If you make the words correctly go to 154.
If you do not, go to 70.

## 153.

You are nearly there. The path seems to emerge from the trees. Check your syllable sticks. If you can get 3 of the following words correct you can go to 98. If you make a mistake – 9.

Egypt _____

supervisor _____

circumstantial _____

gradual _____

## 154.

As you leave the stream behind and carry on through the garden you notice a hedge on the left. The bottom of the hedge is covered in fallen leaves. You seem to see a shape there. Ahead the path is clear.

Will you look under the hedge – 83.
Carry on ahead – 99.

## 155.

The rocky wall shifts to one side revealing three paths. Which will you choose?

Left          16.
Straight on    15.
Right          156.

# 156.

The land gives way to a rocky path. Ahead lies the main peak of Mount Phonic, the Wizard's lair. The path narrows and winds upward. It ends suddenly at the mountainside. There must be a secret door into the mountain. As is always the case with secret doors into mountains you need to say the magic words.

You can do this by writing down (on a separate sheet of paper) as many words as you can that can be made from the word EARTH. You can use any letters to make words of 2 or more letters, e.g. RAT, ARE

You must find at least 15 words before you can find the secret door!

If you succeed – 171.
If you fail, remain here for ever!

# 157.

The bolts of the wizard's SUFFIX energy have weakened you. You are trembling and sweating but you feel the sword's vitality feeding you. The wizard has taken some heavy blows, but casts another bolt of energy; a different kind which sizzles through the air. You slash at the energy with your sword. The sword flashes and the runes (rules) on its blade change to "If the root word ends in magic e, drop the e if the suffix begins with a vowel". Now fight!

| | | |
|---|---|---|
| close+ed | = | closed |
| make+ing | = | _____ |
| amuse+ing | = | _____ |
| nerve+ous | = | _____ |
| love+ly | = | _____ |
| save+ed | = | _____ |
| use+ful | = | _____ |
| price+less | = | _____ |
| clothe+ing | = | _____ |
| tire+ed | = | _____ |

8 or 9 correct – 11
7 or less – 5.

# Battle With The Wizard

## 158.

You approach the skeleton, all that remains of a previous victim. You find a bow with a set of arrows. Write them on your equipment list. These are PREFIX arrows. You take them with you – 149.

## 159.

The bats are too quick for you. They zoom at you, the (ē) piercing your being. You feel your lips and teeth draw back into an (ē) – you become a homophone bat yourself. What a bore! You'd better go back and try again.

## 160.

You draw your sword and hack at the beast. The end of the monster, its tail, is sliced off by your sword. However, its mouth and body still work and you are swallowed by its syllable teeth. (Try again) – 85.

## 161.

The woods thin out and a clearing lies ahead of you. You step on to the grass and a trapdoor gives way. You manage to stop yourself falling into a pit of hissing vowel digraph snakes. You realise that you are still in the maze. The clearing is full of hidden pits. You have to find a path by filling in the pits.

Complete these words by choosing either spelling of (ow), (oi) or (or) **sounds** and writing in the correct spellings. One of the sentences has a clue for you – copy out number 2!

1. A L____d s____nd came from the c____.

2. Do not sp____l or destr____ the castle gate.

3. The lion struck with his p____ before I could p____se for breath.

4. I f____nd the c____n which the b____ had lost.

If you put the words in correctly – 126.
If you do not – 60.

## 162.

You take out the bow and with lightning speed fire your arrows into the heart of the creatures. To see if you win the battle you must choose which word to write next to the clues, using the prefixes shown. One is done for you.

1.  unpopular        not sure _____

2.  uncertain        not well liked <u>unpopular</u>

3.  unfair        not healthy _____

4.  unlucky        not just or honest_____

5.  unfit        when things go wrong_____

6.  misfortune        an error_____

7.  mischief        bad luck_____

8.  misbehave        getting up to tricks_____

9.  mistake        unhappy_____

10. miserable        being naughty_____

If you choose the correct words – 3.
If not – 130.

## 163.

Your hand cannot grip. The ground sucks you into its horrible sludge with a slurping noise! Ugh! you choke to death. Back to 149, to try again.

## 164.

You pull the lever and with a clank and groan the gate rises. A tall figure appears. It is dressed in a long dark robe and hood. You cannot see its face in the hood. It looks empty. It is the PHANTOM. It says "Welcome to END CASTLE! Here you have a night's rest and food, but if you are ever to leave the castle you must first outwit me in a duel of word endings. First you must dine".

You follow the figure who leads you to a huge dining hall. The table is set with a feast to delight the eye (and stomach). You fall upon the food hungrily. After you have dined, and indeed drunken deeply of the wine, the figure booms "Now! To the challenge!"

Have you the wits or has your eating and drinking befuddled your senses? To find out – 104.

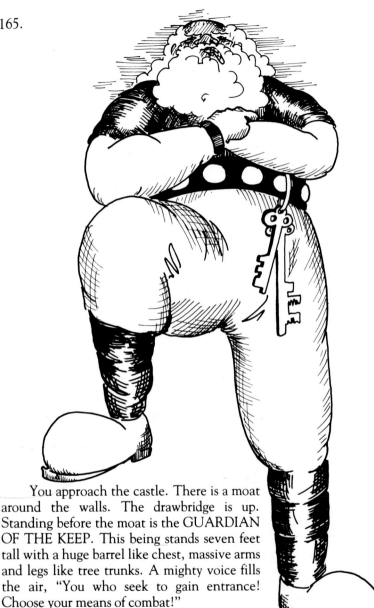

165.

You approach the castle. There is a moat around the walls. The drawbridge is up. Standing before the moat is the GUARDIAN OF THE KEEP. This being stands seven feet tall with a huge barrel like chest, massive arms and legs like tree trunks. A mighty voice fills the air, "You who seek to gain entrance! Choose your means of combat!"

You can choose one of two kinds of unusual spellings. The keeper advances towards you, make your choice:

ph saying (f) go to 115
ch saying (k) go to 125.

## 166.

You remember hearing that Magic e oil is often hidden in caves. You sail past the beach and search the cliffs – 45.

## 167.

You walk along the path. You come to a house. You knock at the door. A witch asks you in for tea.

Do you
a) Go in – 14.
b) Attack her – 25.

## 168.

The sword sinks out of sight and you hear the words "You have failed. The sword cannot be yours!" – 84.

## 169.

You push and shove at the bushes. They scratch you. If only you could slash at them with a knife! The huge thorns seem like sound pictures. If only you can make them into spellings. Beware! They are difficult irregular spellings. Write the correct spelling of the sound picture in the spaces.

We went on a (rŭf) _____ sea crossing.

The road went (strāt) _____ up the hill.

We will (clīm) _____ the mountains.

A puppy is a (yŭng) _____ dog.

We went down to the beach to see the ship (rĕk) _____.

What (dŭs) _____ he do for a living.

If you spelt all the words correctly – 133.
If not then – 112.

The garden is very well laid out, with a lawn and walls all around. There is a strange feel to the air. Suddenly there is a "clunk!" You turn around and there is a wall behind you! You are trapped! There are walls on all four sides.

Will you try to climb the walls – 94.
or use a spell – 148.

## 171.

A door in the side of the mountain opens. A dark passage leads into the mountain. You walk into the dark entrance. A dank smell greets you! It is a pity you cannot see. You will have to throw some light on the matter. To do this you need to rearrange the letters to make a word, using the clues given. They are igh (ī) or ch words.

It comes after day – tighn = night

Something you eat with fish – ipchs = _____

He wears shining armour – tnighk = _____

A head cook – fech = _____

You eyes have it – tighs = _____

Some things you need in this dark entrance!

chort   tligh = _____   _____

Right – 183.
Wrong – 173.

## 172.

You turn upstream. The dark water winds upwards through a narrow way. The oily looking water seems strangely quiet. You see a white shape gloating down towards you.

Will you investigate – 175.
or go on – 185.

# 173.

You lose your way in the dark, and stumble over the edge of an underground cliff. Your screams can be heard fading into the distance. A pity to end on such a note! You manage to grab hold of a ledge and try again at 171.

# 174.

You set off downstream. The water flows slowly at first, then picks up speed. The torch shows a quick current and you hear a roaring sound ahead. Suddenly the river ends in a huge waterfall. The river tumbles over the edge of a high cliff. Down below you see a huge underground cavern. It is lit by glowing lights like small suns set into the rock roof. It is the VILLAGE OF LETTERS. The scene is laid out like a map before you.

Now go to 177.

# 175.

You stop and cast a pebble at the shape. The shape rears up and swims towards you with amazing speed.

What can it be? 176.

# 176.

Oh dear! you have disturbed the great BLIND WHITE CROCODILE. It is blind and white from generations in the underground dark. However, it tracks its prey by smell, and you are its prey. It slithers and slimes towards you, its huge jaws and sharp teeth gnashing together with a lust for your flesh!

Your sword is useless in the confined space. You grab a piece of driftwood. You only hope is to jam it into the jaws of the beast. You can do this by putting a circle around the words that start with the sound (j).

over→

| | | | |
|---|---|---|---|
| glove | gentle | guy | gym |
| genius | grape | giraffe | gasp |
| gypsy | germ | gash | gyrate |
| giant | grub | gent | |

If you got them all correct – 193.
If not – 180.


## 177.

Before you can explore the area you must brave the waterfall. You see a small boat by the river. You get in and steer towards the falls. The river shoots you out into space in your flimsy craft. Was this a wise thing to do? Whether you survive or not depends on your ability to read 'ea'. ea has 3 sounds (ĕ), (ē) and (ā). Read these words and write the sound pictures that ea makes:

| | |
|---|---|
| dream (ē) | bread _____ |
| deaf _____ | great _____ |
| steak _____ | spread _____ |
| leaf _____ | mean _____ |
| break _____ | feather _____ |

If you were correct – 186.
If you made mistakes – 181.


## 178.

You nibble on the MAGICAL MUSHROOM. Your magical sight shows you the start passage out of the mountain cave. You follow it for a short while. There is a huge door here. Check your equipment list.

If you have the Clue Key – 182.
If you do not – 187 and look for it somewhere else. (The Pit?)

# 179.

The weight of water is too great. Your foot slips on a rock. You tumble over and this time you are not so lucky. Your brains and other internal organs lie splattered on the rocks below. A real shame! Go back and try again! – 195.

# 180.

The jaws of the crocodile crunch through your bones. A painful death, although the crocodile is pleased. It has not had such a feast for years! You can try again at 183.

# 181.

Your puny boat smashes to pieces on the rocks below. You also smash to pieces – bad luck, try again – 177.

# 182.

You take the Clue Key. You put the key into the lock. A message appears on the door.

"*All* and *full*, when used as a prefix or suffix lose an l. For example

all + most – almost
beauty + full – beautiful"

Now complete the following:

| | |
|---|---|
| _____ways | Wonder_____ |
| _____most | help_____ |
| _____so | use_____ |
| _____though | care_____ |

If you fail you stay in the gloom forever!

If you get them all correct the door opens with a creak. You see a glimmer of light at the end of the tunnel. You walk towards it and find yourself on the mountainside – 137.

## 183.

The light of your torch casts flickering shadows in the gloomy tunnel. Damp rocks lie ahead of you, and you see the gleam of reflected light on water. It is a river flowing across your path. You decide to follow it.

Will you go downstream? – 174.
or upstream? – 172.

## 184.

The CAVE WRAITH fades into the air. You approach the book and, blowing the dust off its black leather cover, you see a title in gold letters "THE BOOK OF PLURALS". Write this down on your equipment list. To consult the book at any time go to 203. (Make a note of the page number)

To return to the pool, and further places, climb out of the cave to 187.

## 185.

You walk on up river. As your back is turned the white shape looms up behind you. What is it? Go to 176.

## 186.

You puny boat smashes to pieces on the rocks below. Luckily you fall out of the boat on the way down and miss the rocks. You land in a deep pool. Although you plunge into the icy depths you fight your way to the surface and crawl to the shore gasping. You can now explore the area and seek the Wizard so that you can destroy him – 187.

There are many place to explore. You will need to visit most of these in search of magical things that will help you to defeat the Wizard. Sometimes you will have to visit a place more than once as you will be sent back here to collect equipment elsewhere before you can go on.

This is the final and most dangerous stage of the Word Quest. The Wizard is very powerful, and has many wicked helpers who will try and thwart your progress, so be extra careful.

You may explore
1). The Cave – 188.
2). The Village – 204.
3). The Mushroom Forest – 198.
4). The Pit – 189.
5). The Crack in the Wall – 212.

## 188.

You walk around the pool, a rocky shoreline with the mist and spray of the waterfall soaking your skin. The waterfall forms a large sheet of water in front of the cliffside.

Will you
1). Climb up the rocks to the cliff – 195.
2). Explore elsewhere – 187.

## 189.

You set off across the open plain. In the distance you see steam and red glowing lights flashing in the rocks. Suddenly with a loud crack, boiling HOT LAVA spews out of the crevice. The heat from liquid rock singes your hair. You run! Can you escape. Write oi or oy to complete these words:

___l

j___nt

b___

v___age

n___se

r___al

ann___

t___

av___d

destr___

If you succeed – 196.
If you fail – 192.

## 190.

The ungrateful BEAST crunches you up for dinner. (Go back to 211 and try again)

## 191.

You walk through the forest. The fungus thickens. You can't find a path. You stumble about and touch your leg against a purple and green mushroom. It stings violently and you notice a large rash spreading. It is a very poisonous mushroom. Retrace your steps quickly before you get a lethal dose of the poison – 187.

Hint: Don't come back to the forest until you have found a guide – try the village.

## 192.

The terrible heat of the molten LAVA saps your speed. You trip and fall. Just before you die you smell the burning flesh of your own legs as the blazing fiery LAVA swallows you up feet first! A particularly nasty death! Go back to 189 and try again.

## 193.

The wood jams in its jaws. The crocodile writhes in agony and slithers off into the river. It is not happy but then you cannot please everyone all of the time. You plod on upstream. The river narrows to a gushing torrent spouting out of a hole in the mountain wall. No way through here. Back to 183.

## 194.

The WISE ONES scream their anger at being outwitted. In their excitement they overturn an oil lamp. The flames leap up the straw walls of the hut and catch the dry bodies of the WISE ONES. You run for the door. One of the WISE ONES begs to come with you, hanging on to your arm.

Will you thrust him back into the flames – 209.
or let him come with you – 202.

You climb the rocks. They are slippery with moss and slime. You plunge your body under the waterfall. The force of water throws you off balance. You must match the abbreviations table with their complete words. One has been done for you.

| | |
|---|---|
| I'll _____ | I will |
| We've _____ | It is |
| Can't _____ | Could not |
| It's _____ | they have |
| Isn't _____ | is not |
| Won't _____ | We have |
| We'll _____ | She is |
| Couldn't _____ | cannot |
| She's _____ | Will not |
| They've _____ | We will |

If you were correct – 200.
If you made a mistake – 179.


## 196.

You outrun the fiery LAVA. You come to a rather dark area of the cavern. Ahead of you is the PIT, a large black hole into the solid rock floor. You peer over the edge. The walls are sheer and you hear a deep snarling, growling, beastlike noise. It seems to be calling you to help. You notice a rope ladder by the side of the pit, attached at one end by stout metal spikes in the rock floor.

Will you investigate – 205.
Hurry back to look elsewhere – 187.


## 197.

A thick mist seems to fog your sight. You feel even weaker and the chanting of the WISE ONES puts you into a deep sleep. You wake up old and wrinkled – you have become a WISE ONE, puppet of the WIZARD. Go back to 210 and try again.

# 198.

The path you follow becomes overgrown with fungus, and the stench of rotting mould offends your nostrils. Ahead lies a tangle of vast mushroom and toadstool trees. Some are poisonous, and the path is lost in the confusion. It is the MUSHROOM FOREST.

You can go on – 191.
Try and find a guide (try looking in the village) – 187.

# 199.

You go forward and break off a piece of the MAGIC MUSHROOM. Write it on your equipment list. You leave the forest. Your guide disappears – 187.

# 200.

You stagger through the sheet of water and find a secret cave behind the waterfall. The walls of the cave are covered with a glowing moss, but it is warm and reasonably dry inside. At the back of the cave is an old table, and lying on the table is an old black book. As you reach to examine the book a ghostly figure appears out of thin air. It is the CAVE WRAITH. A hollow and sad voice fills the air.

"If ye seek the knowledge of the book, you must first set my soul to rest".

The terrible MIXED PHONIC VOWEL sound of the CAVE WRAITH fills your ears. Once again you must do battle with vowel digraphs.

Look at the letters below. Can you put 2 vowels in each of the spaces shown?

For example gr___n can become grain or green

r_____m  r_____n  gr_____n  p_____l  l_____n

t____d  m_____n  st____l  sp____n  f____l

r____d  b____t  f____t  ch____n

Now try to make real words with the following – ai, ee, ea, oa and oo.

Write the words down underneath here. There are at least 38 possible words. Most of the words use more than one vowel digraph, e.g. grain, green, groan. You can use the examples.

| | | | |
|---|---|---|---|
| ———— | ———— | ———— | ———— |
| ———— | ———— | ———— | ———— |
| ———— | ———— | ———— | ———— |
| ———— | ———— | ———— | ———— |
| ———— | ———— | ———— | ———— |
| ———— | ———— | ———— | ———— |

If you succeed (30 words or more) – 184.
If you fail (less than 30 words) – 206.

## 201.

You draw your Suffix Rule Sword. It hums with power. The BEAST, who now appears to have the light of intelligence in its eye, mutters a spell under its breath. You slash at the BEAST, but with a savage cry it leaps on you, stabbing with its tusks. You are soon to become some more of the bones which lie around the pit! Your only hope is to talk to the BEAST quickly before the power of your sword dies – 211.

## 202.

The wise one is pathetically grateful and clings on to your arm. "I shall be your guide. Come, follow me!" He explains that he was once an adventurer, but became one of the WIZARD's slaves, a fate which you escaped at the village.

You decide to trust the sad creature, and he guides you to the MUSHROOM FOREST – 207.

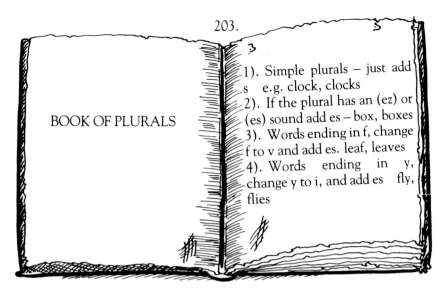

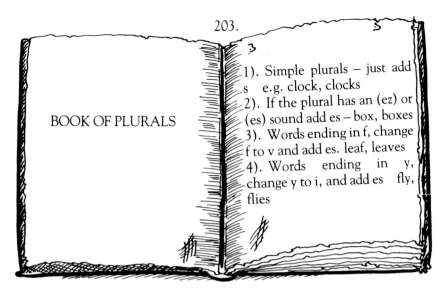**203.**

1). Simple plurals – just add s e.g. clock, clocks
2). If the plural has an (ez) or (es) sound add es – box, boxes
3). Words ending in f, change f to v and add es. leaf, leaves
4). Words ending in y, change y to i, and add es fly, flies

BOOK OF PLURALS

Now go back to where you were.

**204.**

You follow a well trodden path to the village. The pathetic huts cluster in a circle around a larger one. The people are slow and fearful. Many cannot speak, read or write. The WIZARD has stolen their words. You approach the central hut. You enter. Inside is a long bench upon which sit a dozen aged people. Their flesh is sunken and wrinkled. You say "Help me escape the cavern!" As if driven by some outside power their eyes light up and, as one, they chant in a terrible voice

"Where there is none there is some
Where there is one there are two
Where there are some there are more"

What can this mean?

While you ponder this, a strange feeling of weakness begins to overcome you.

Quickly, check your equipment and think what could help you.

Write it here ⎯⎯⎯⎯⎯⎯⎯⎯

Now go to 210.

You hurl one end of the rope ladder over the PIT and climb down. In the dim light you see a massive hairy creature. It has massive tusks set in a black jaw, its eyes glare redly at you, and its massive paws have sharp claws about two inches long. The FINAL SYLLABLE BEAST, (for that is what it is,) towers over you. It has been imprisoned here by the wizard. There is a golden key on a long chain around its neck. The BEAST now lurches towards you with a roar and stretches out a massive paw.

Will you attack the BEAST with your sword – 201.
Try and tame him – 211.

## 206.

The low moaning of the WRAITH drones on and on, driving you mad with despair. You become one of the lesser wraiths, doomed to serve the WRAITH in the cave forever – 200 to try again.

## 207.

The MUSHROOM FOREST is dark, gloomy and smells unpleasantly of rotting mould. The huge mushrooms tower over you. They are multi-coloured – red, yellow, green, purple. Your guide says "Avoid the purple and green mushrooms, they are poisonous, as are the yellow ones". It guides you safely through the trackless forest.

At last you arrive in a small clearing. In the centre is a vast blue mushroom. It is the MAGICAL MUSHROOM. Your guide says "It is said that a person having a bit of the magic mushroom can see hidden paths. Before you can obtain a piece you must piece together these compound words.

One has been done for you.

| | | |
|---|---|---|
| mush yard | Mushroom | |
| news ship | _____ | |
| farm room | _____ | |
| war paper | _____ | |
| him about | _____ | |
| some self | _____ | |
| round thing | _____ | |

If you are correct – 199.
If you make a mistake – 208.

## 208.

You pass on into the forest. The fungus is all around. The path is nowhere to be seen. You lose all track of time and direction, stumbling aimlessly about. Soon you tire and sit down to catch your breath. It is a pity that you lie back on a purple and green toadstool. Its poison is very deadly. One touch on the skin is all that it needs. You die a painful death. (Go back to 207 and try again).

You push him into the burning hut, his cry of despair rings in your ears – You can't bear it and pull him out of the flames – 202.

## 210.

Well? You should have written the Book of Plurals. Read the WISE ONES' chant and you will see why. If you have not got the Book of Plurals on your equipment list you must go and search in the Cave – back to 187.

If you have the book of plurals write the plurals for the following words. You would be wise to consult the Book!

| | |
|---|---|
| hand _____ | crab _____ |
| house _____ | calf _____ |
| berry _____ | scarf _____ |
| lunch _____ | lorry _____ |
| thief _____ | fox _____ |
| cherry _____ | door _____ |

If you were correct – 194.
If you made mistakes – 197.

## 211.

You speak soothing words at the BEAST and a gleam of understanding is seen in its eyes. The BEAST appears intelligent and stretches out its paw further, whimpering. You see a large thorn which you pluck out. The BEAST croaks in a harsh voice "Thank you! I shall not kill you immediately. If you can solve my final syllable riddles, I will let you free".

"cian" at the end of a word is often used where it is the name of a person with a skill or job. Here are some example:

musician magician politician
electrician optician technician

Now write the correct ones against these clues

1). Skilled in magic _____

2). Seller of glasses (spectacles) _____

3). User of technical knowledge _____

4). Dealer in electrical equipment _____

5). Player of music _____

6). Takes part in politics _____

If you are correct – 213.
If you made mistakes – 190.

## 212.

You arrive at the crack in the wall. There is an odd shaped rock here. Check your equipment list. If you have a piece of MAGICAL MUSHROOM you may go to 178. If you do not – back to 187 and look elsewhere.

## 213.

The beast gives you the Golden Key from around his neck. You depart, climbing up the rope ladder. Write down the key, (it is the Clue Key) on your equipment list, then you make your way back to the pool – 187.

## 214.

You draw out your syllable sticks. Make sure you have read about them at 77.

Will you take both Red and Green – 113.
Only one stick – 105.

# 215.

You step easily through the gap in the undergrowth. Suddenly the ground beneath you gives way. You feel yourself being dragged down into a syllable sand. The marshy ground has you in its grip and your only hope is to grasp the mangrove roots and pull yourself out.

To do this you must put together the floating syllable bits around you to make solid ground (real words). One syllable from each column.

Two examples have been done for you:

| la  | tol | label  |
|-----|-----|--------|
| pis | bel | pistol |
| vel | sin | _____ |
| but | vet | _____ |
| ba  | ter | _____ |
| pen | lip | _____ |
| tu  | cil | _____ |

If you manage to make 5 real words – 134.
If you fail – 163.


# 216.

You manage to escape – 126.


# 217.

The noise deafens you. You are driven mad by the (a) sound.


# 218.

You haven't got any magic e oil because you tried to attack the witch. You visit her and apologise. She is really very nice and gives you tea and a small bottle of Magic e oil. (Go back to 10 and use it's magic to cross the river.)

## 219.

You look round and see that your monster is beckoning you towards the ditch – 159.

## 220.

Syllable sticks can be got from a special kind of tree. You should have met the tree. Go to 35. If you succeed you will be given syllable sticks. Then go back to 214.

## 221.

You did not make enough words at the beginning of the adventure with the spider and crow blends. Go to 53, and make at least 10 words.

## 222.

In the icy water of the ditch is a GNOME. To escape the GNOME you need to use the clues to think of "GN" words (all these words have a silent G).

A small ugly elf-like man _____

A small flying insect that bites _____

Grinding your teeth together _____

Chewing, for example, on a bone _____

If you were correct you may carry on – 96.
If not die here in the ditch!

Well done brave adventurer! You have defeated the wizard. You have done well, it has been a long and difficult task. You can be very proud of yourself. All the secrets of the words are yours. As a bonus, all the gold, jewels and other treasure are yours. Beware others will be after it, but that is another adventure!